Basix

Rock Drum Method

Patrick Wilson

It's not easy learning a musical instrument, even for those who seem to have a natural ability or talent. It takes time to develop skills through practice and patience. While playing rock drums may seem easier than, perhaps, keyboard or guitar, it takes real dedication to become a virtuoso!

The ideal situation in learning any instrument is to find a great teacher. Very, very few of today's awesome players made it without someone's help. If you find you really love playing drums, you'll also find a way to study with an experienced drummer who has talent and the ability to help you do what you love: laying down great grooves and monster drives!

ABOUT THE CD

The CD that is available with the book features play-along pieces, so you can learn without having all your musician friends come over, watching and waiting while you work on playing! The right channel of the recording can be turned off, which has the drum track. Look for the CD logo throughout the book . . . it indicates where there are companion recorded examples!

Tracks 1–12

Play Now!

The opening of the optional CD (Tracks 1–12) does not require use of the book. By just listening, it will take you step-by-step through the instruction needed to play a simple rock beat in less than 20 minutes! By the end of this session, you will be ready to play along with studio musicians laying down a basic rock beat!!!

Featured drummer: Dave Tull
Keyboards: Greg Hilfman
Bass: Tre Henry
Guitar: Steve Hall

Cover photo courtesy of Yamaha Corporation of America

CONTENTS

PART I Getting Into Gear

HOW TO PLAY BASIX™

SETTING UP

Pages 56–58 show how drumset components are positioned relative to one another. Some drum and cymbal manufacturers have literature available which shows various artists' setups. It is your decision as to how you place the instruments, depending not only on the instruments you have, but also on *personal preference and comfort.* This is the key. What may be good for a drummer you idolize may not be right for you.

All the instruments should be easily reachable. Your kit should be centralized to minimize reaching, stretching and twisting. Hardware enables you to tilt or angle the instruments to *your* liking. Take advantage of this! As you begin to play and gradually improve, chances are that you will find better ways to position the instruments.

GET A GRIP!

There are two grips commonly used: traditional and matched. One is not "better" than the other. The traditional grip is more common among jazz drummers and those players who come from a more "traditional" background.* On the other hand (no pun intended!), the matched grip evolved from rock players in the '60s.

It has been argued that the traditional grip allows more finesse while the matched grip offers more power. As a result, nearly all hard rockers choose the matched grip. You may wish to experiment, but understand there are drummers who use both grips, depending on their needs at the moment.

Some switch grips while playing! The choice is yours . . . there is no right or wrong decision. Since the matched grip is more useful in rock and is learned more naturally, you may want to go with that. Both grips are presented so you may experiment.

▲ *Traditional grip.*

▲ *Matched grip.*

* This often implies a study of *rudiments.* (Rudiments are specific, standardized exercises that build technique, endurance and strength, while giving the drummer "licks," which can be applied to playing.) For further study, *International Drum Rudiments* by Rob Carson and Jay Wanamaker contains all drum rudiments.

HOW TO PLAY BASIX™
(continued)

THE RIGHT HAND
Traditional & Matched Grip

Whether you choose traditional or matched grip, the right hand is the same.

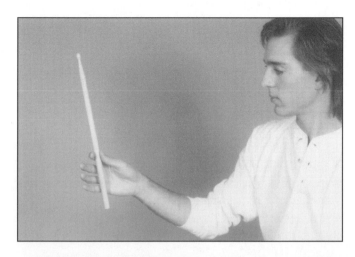

Hold the stick between your thumb and index finger about 5 inches from the back end of the stick. The stick should be parallel to your palm. The index finger should naturally curve around the stick.

Allow the remaining fingers to curve in a relaxed manner around the stick (as with the index finger). They should not completely close around the stick, but should gently rest against it. Nothing should feel forced, but should seem relaxed and fairly natural.

With your palm facing parallel to the floor, the right hand should look like this.

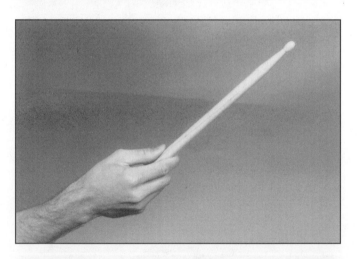

With your palm facing up, the grip should look like this.

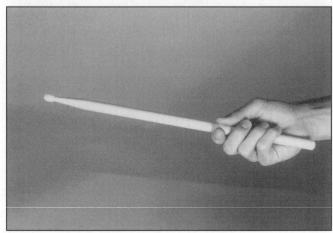

THE LEFT HAND—
Traditional Grip

With the hand perpendicular to the floor, hold the stick with the thumb in the "pocket" (between your thumb and first finger) about two inches from the butt end of the stick.

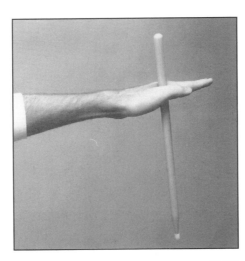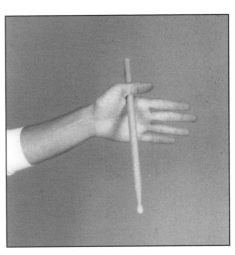

Close your ring finger and little finger, then turn the palm up, allowing the stick to lie on the ring finger. The thumb should curve a bit.

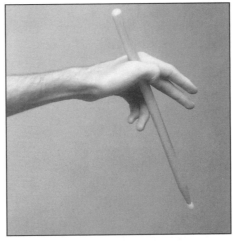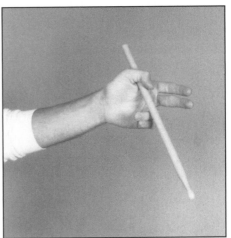

Allow the middle finger and index finger to curve over the stick naturally. Keep the hand relaxed!

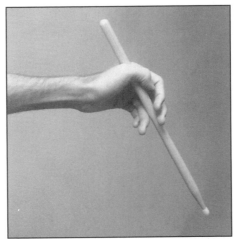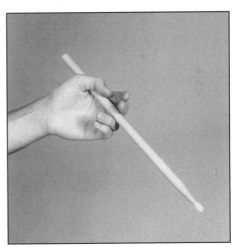

THE LEFT HAND—
Matched Grip

The left hand will "match" (as the name of the grip implies) the right.

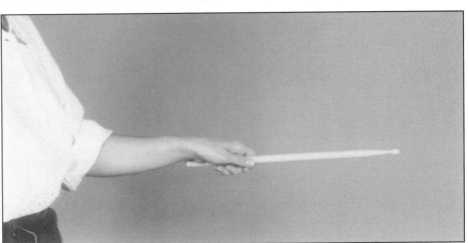

USING YOUR GRIP—THE WRIST

When playing, the action is made primarily with the wrist. (The fingers play a significant role, but that comes a bit later.) **Very little arm motion is needed**. Even when playing loud, little arm motion is necessary. Certain styles of drumming—heavy metal, for instance—promote movement for visual effect. If that's what you're into, great!—but realize it isn't required.

The most important concept here is to STAY RELAXED! Try to be very conscious of when your arms, wrists and fingers become tense . . . then, back off! It *is* possible to damage tendons if you do not learn to stay relaxed while playing.

THE RIGHT-HAND WRIST MOTION
Matched & Traditional

1) Without tapping on any surface, bend at the wrist so the stick moves upward.

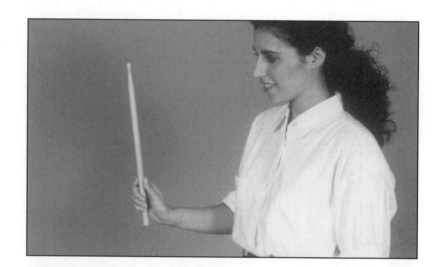

2) Relax the wrist, allowing the stick to drop parallel to the floor.

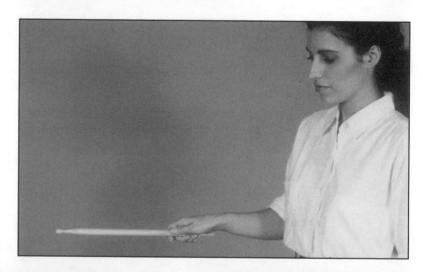

Now repeat #1 and #2 a few times. The stick should move straight up and down. It shouldn't "slice" at an angle.

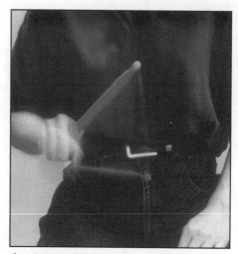

▲ *The* **RIGHT** *way—Straight up and down movement.*

▲ *The* **WRONG** *way—slicing at an angle.*

THE LEFT-HAND WRIST MOTION

Matched

Identical to the motion used in the right hand (see previous page).

Traditional

1) Without tapping on any surface, rotate the wrist less than a quarter turn bringing the stick tip up a few inches.

2) Rotate the wrist back to its original position bringing the stick downward.

Now repeat #1 and #2 a few times. As with the right hand, the stick should move straight up and down and should not be moving at an angle (see bottom of previous page). Because the grip with this hand is less natural than with the right, it may take some practice achieving a straight up and down stick motion with comfort, while keeping the wrist, hand and fingers relaxed.

Now, let's try it on a drum!

USING YOUR GRIP— THE FINGERS

Seated at your drumset, repeat the exercises on the previous two pages for your particular grip as follows. This time, however, hit your snare rather than just move the sticks in the air.

R = right hand

1.

L = left hand

2.

(alternating hands)

3.

You will notice that there is a natural tendency for the stick to bounce back when you hit the drum. It is no different from the way a ball bounces. If you drop a basketball, gravity pulls it down, then it rebounds back up. You don't have to pull the ball up; it naturally occurs.

This is how drums are played. You need force (a bit of muscle along with gravity) to get the stick moving down—almost none when playing soft!—then simply "catch it" on the rebound. This is where the fingers come into play. They act to catch the stick on the rebound about 2 inches above the drumhead. Let's look at each hand . . .

◀ *Danny Elfman*
Photo: Amy Lehman © 1995

As frontman and main musical force of Oingo Boingo, Danny Elfman used a combination of unique instrumentation, odd rhythmic patterns and unusual lyrical content to constantly engage and challenge his listeners.

THE RIGHT-HAND FINGERS

With the upstroke, the fingers should release the stick.

They remain this way until the moment after the stick hits the surface. Then, the fingers quickly close to catch the stick as it completes the rebound.

THE LEFT-HAND FINGERS

Matched

Identical to the motion used in the right hand.

Traditional

In similar fashion to the concept with the right hand, the index and middle fingers release the stick with the upstroke. The stick no longer rests on the ring finger. It is "airborne," held only by the thumb.

Just after the stick hits the surface, the wrist turns back to

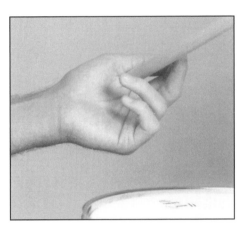 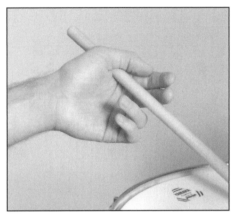

its original position (about 2 inches above the drumhead) and the ring finger resumes contact while the index and middle fingers curl back to catch the stick.

This action must become natural with each hand so it occurs without having to think about it. The only way to achieve this is through practice.

Chops Builder

INTRODUCTION TO THE SINGLE-STROKE ROLL

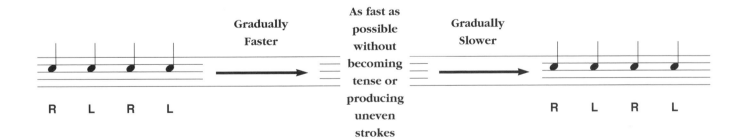

Gradually Faster → As fast as possible without becoming tense or producing uneven strokes → Gradually Slower →

R L R L   R L R L

While it may seem elementary, this is a very important exercise because you are laying the foundation for your technique. Keep the strokes even. Remember, *always stay relaxed!*

HOW TO READ MUSIC

Why read music? There *are* talented drummers who do not read music. The late big-band drummer Buddy Rich was one of them. He listened to his band play an arrangement once or twice, then sat down and pretty much had it figured out. (His talent and ability to memorize was exceptional!) All drummers learn to a significant degree about playing by watching and listening.

For purposes of learning from a book, it is necessary to communicate ideas through written music. Learning this language, like any language, takes a little effort and practice. **The advantage is that you will have an added skill that others may not**. If you wish to play beyond your own enjoyment—in a band, for example—you will be a step ahead of others. You will have basic music reading skills, which will be an advantage when communicating with other musicians who also read music or in getting work!

SYMBOLS FOR SOUNDS—NOTES

| Whole Note (Semibreve) | Half Note (Minim) | Quarter Note (Crotchet) | Eighth Note (Quaver) | Sixteenth Note (Semiquaver) |

Each of the above characters symbolizes sound. The difference between them is duration, or length. A half note is half the length of a whole note, a quarter is one-quarter the length of a whole, an eighth is one-eighth of a whole, etc.—that is why they are named as such.

SYMBOLS FOR SILENCE—RESTS

| Whole Rest (Semibreve Rest) | Half Rest (Minim Rest) | Quarter Rest (Crotchet Rest) | Eighth Rest (Quaver Rest) | Sixteenth Rest (Semiquaver Rest) |

Each of the above characters, called rests, symbolizes silence. In terms of length or duration, they correspond to the notes. A whole rest is equal in length to a whole note, a half note equal to a half rest, and so on.

Simply speaking, all music is composed of these two types of symbols: notes and rests (or sound and silence). These are the symbols you actually read as you play written music.

THE FRAMEWORK

In order to make music, it is necessary to place notes and rests on a type of roadmap. We call this roadmap the **staff** (stave). The staff consists of five horizontal lines.

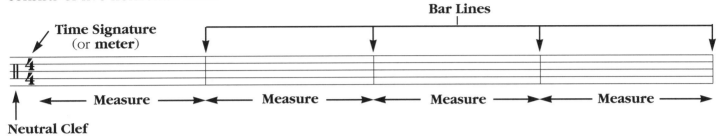

The vertical lines which divide the staff into sections are **bar lines**. The divided sections are known as **measures** or **bars**. The two short vertical lines at the very beginning form the **neutral clef** used for non-pitched music and needs no further explanation here. The stacked numbers at the beginning of the staff are the **time signature,** sometimes called **meter**.

The time signature is of special significance. The *top number* represents the number of beats in one measure (in this case, 4 beats per measure). The *bottom number* indicates the type of note or rest that will get *one* beat. In this case, 4 = a quarter note or rest. If the bottom number were an 8, it would signify a eighth note or rest; if it were a 2, it would mean a half note or rest, etc.

Various Time Signatures:

How many beats? _____   _____   _____   _____

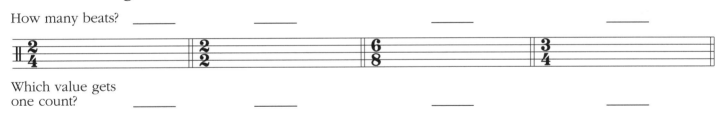

Which value gets
one count?   _____   _____   _____   _____

For each of the above time signatures, how many beats are there in each bar? What note or rest value gets one count? (Review the third paragraph on this page if there is any question in your mind.) After you're sure of the answers, check them at the bottom of this page.

In order to better understand the concept of a time signature, let's look at some simple examples of music on the next page.

Answers: 2/4—2 beats per bar, quarter note or rest gets 1 count; 2/2—2 beats per bar, half note or rest gets 1 count; 6/8—6 beats per bar, eighth note or rest gets 1 count; 3/4—3 beats per bar, quarter note or rest gets 1 count.

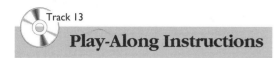

Track 13

Play-Along Instructions

READING YOUR FIRST LINES OF MUSIC

In Ex. 1, there are 4 beats in each measure. There can be 4 quarter rests, 4 quarter notes or combinations of quarter notes and rests—but there can only be 4 types of quarter configurations total. The next line of music (Ex. 2) includes 3 quarter notes or rests in each bar. The third example (Ex. 3) is made up of 2 quarter notes or rests per bar.

Count evenly aloud ("one... two... three... four... one... two... three... four...") as indicated above Ex. 1. As you count, tap on your snare drum when there is a note below the number; do nothing (except continue counting) when there is a rest. Try it several times until you feel somewhat comfortable.

Track 14

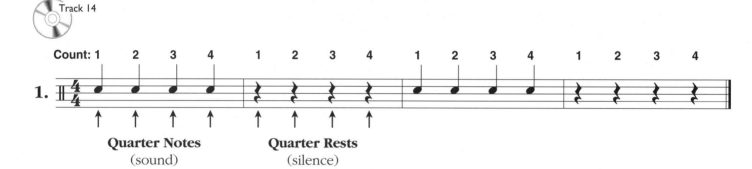

Track 15

Try the next line (Ex. 2). This time you'll be counting in patterns of three, tapping on your snare each time a quarter note appears below. Again, do this several times until you get the hang of it.

Track 16

The third line (Ex. 3) is a bit different because you rest on the first count. Also, notice that this line has six measures, rather than four.

Track 17

The last line (Ex. 4) is also a bit tricky, but should be fun. Like the first line, you'll be counting in four again.

USING YOUR FEET

Surprisingly, there are different ways to approach playing with your feet. The technique you use may influence how you adjust your throne.

FLAT TECHNIQUE

The foot lies flat on the pedal at all times. In a resting position, the hi-hat is open or the bass drum beater "cocked" away from the head. To play, pressure is applied to the entire foot. In the case of the bass drum, it is preferable to allow the beater to return to the cocked position immediately after striking the head.

TOE TECHNIQUE

In a resting position, pressure is applied to the pedal with the toe end of the foot—the hi-hat remains closed; the bass drum beater rests against the head. The heel doesn't touch the pedal. To play, the entire leg lifts slightly, bouncing on the ball of the foot. Many drummers who use this have their throne adjusted a little higher. This technique is especially useful when playing faster rhythms. Also, this can produce more power and, therefore, is the common choice of rock drummers.

HEEL & TOE ("ROCKING") TECHNIQUE

This is usually associated with the hi-hat. As the name implies, the foot rocks back and forth. First, the toe end of the foot presses into the pedal and the heel comes off the pedal. Then, the heel comes down as the toe end of the foot rises, so the foot actually moves like the base of a rocking chair. This technique, while not useful for fast music, is very comfortable for keeping an even pace for other, not-so-fast tunes, especially moderate jazz (swing).

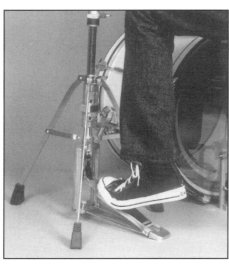
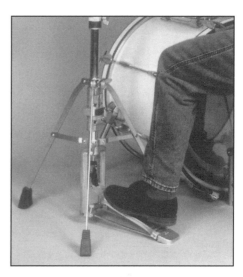

CHOOSING A TECHNIQUE

As with choosing grips, there is no right or wrong pedal technique. The flat technique utilizes economy of motion in the case of the bass drum because the beater doesn't have to be brought back in a position ready to strike—it is already there. But there are players—many of whom are "rockers"—who swear by the toe technique. You may want to try each for a while, then go with what you prefer. Or you may wish to use both or a sort of hybrid.

Try the following exercises using the three techniques mentioned above. Play them several times until you feel somewhat comfortable with each.

Paul Hester (Crowded House) ▶
Photo: Amy Lehman © 1995

Crowded House exemplified the classic 1980s pop-trio, and Paul Hester's smooth, understated drumming helped drive the band's crisp, original sound.

THE LINES & SPACES—
WHERE INSTRUMENTS ARE INDICATED

The purpose in having lines and spaces on the staff in drum music is to indicate which instruments to play. (Pitched instruments, such as a guitar or piano, use the lines and spaces to determine what pitches to play.) The following shows where each instrument on your drumset is placed on the staff:

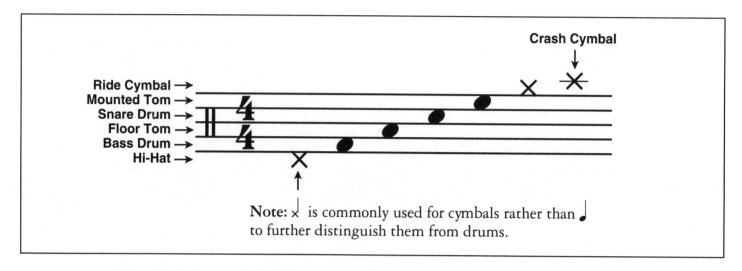

READING THE LINES & SPACES

In the following exercises you will be playing all the instruments on your set. It will take some time to get used to which instrument to play. At first, the instruments are marked in parenthesis. Use whichever hand seems most natural. (All the hi-hat and bass drum notes should be played with the foot unless otherwise indicated.)

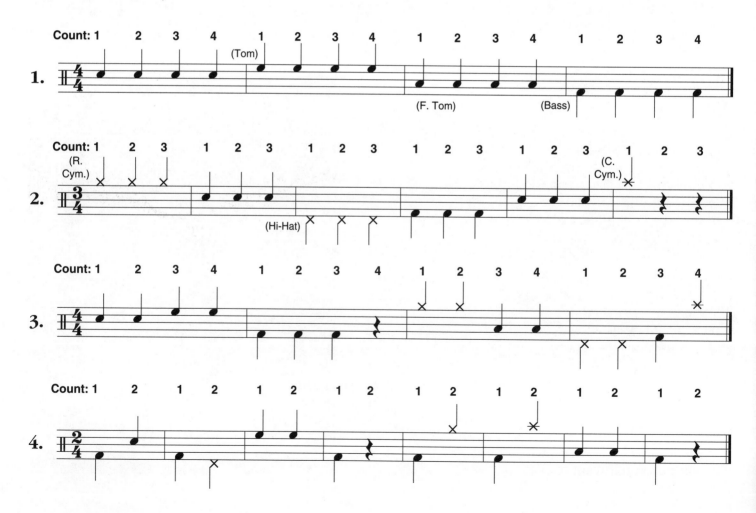

WHERE TO PLAY

WITH THE STICK

There are a few areas of the stick that are commonly referred to in other books, magazines and elsewhere. While the vast majority of playing is done with the tip, the shoulder and the butt of the stick are sometimes used.

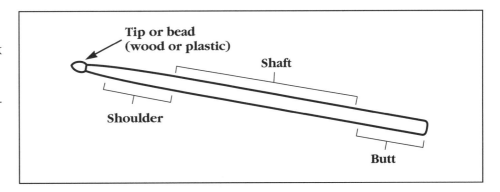

ON THE DRUMHEAD

Depending upon where you strike the drumhead, you can produce different sounds. Playing near the rim produces a thin, high-pitched sound; playing at the center produces a full-bodied sound. Ordinarily, drummers play slightly off center, about an inch or two. But don't forget that different sounds are valuable assets that will enable you to create the unique "feel" and sound character you're looking for by mixing various tone colors in your playing.

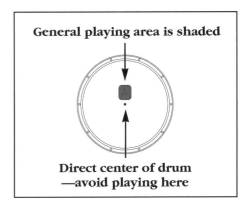

ON THE CYMBAL

The parts of the cymbal are few, but the areas upon which to play are many. Some progressive drummers even utilize the edge in a special manner—by striking it with the stick perpendicular (at a 90-degree angle).

Generally, the ride cymbal is played with the tip of the stick about 2 inches from the edge. The shoulder of the drum stick may be used for accents or contrast, playing on the shoulder, edge or bell.

The crash cymbal is most often played with a glancing blow across the edge of the cymbal with the shoulder of the stick. However, you may find other techniques and playing areas, as with the ride cymbal, that provide sounds you'll want to use.

Never be afraid to experiment and try unusual ideas.

Playing on the bell of a cymbal creates a "ping" sound somewhat like a high-pitched cowbell. As a result, it is used in Latin and African rhythms, but also as a driving pulse in rock when played with the shoulder or butt end of the stick. (When practicing exercises you can try playing on the bell of the cymbal to achieve a different effect.)

Try to identify the bell sound in recordings, making note of how it is used within the music and the effect it creates.

For a thorough understanding of cymbals, you may wish to purchase *Cymbals: A Crash Course* by Mitchell Peters and Dave Black.

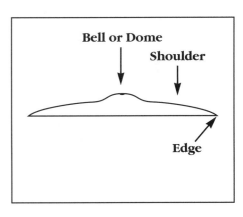

PART II The Basix™

THE PACE OF MUSIC—TEMPO

The staff serves as a kind of road map to read music. The goal is to get from one place to another—in this case, from the beginning of the music to the end. As explained, we first must look at the time signature before we begin to know how many beats are in a measure and what kind of note or rest gets one beat.

Then, as we begin the journey, we travel at an even pace. This pace is known as **tempo**. It is the pulse or beat of music. When an audience claps along to music at a concert, they are naturally feeling the beat or tempo. You probably have found yourself tapping your foot many times to music you enjoy.

▲ *Slim Jim Phantom* (Stray Cats) Photo: Amy Lehman © 1995

As drummer of the 1980s retro-rockabilly trio Stray Cats, Slim Jim Phantom kept it straightforward and simple, playing a stripped-down kick-snare set while standing up during performances.

Before you begin playing any music, you must have the tempo in mind. This is why a musician counts to other musicians before beginning to play. In this manner, everyone knows the tempo before the music starts. The drummer is always in charge of maintaining a steady, even tempo, though it is also the responsibility of the other musicians. For this reason, the drummer is often called the "time keeper."

FINDING THE RIGHT TEMPO— THE METRONOME

There is a device that should be used to determine tempos: a **metronome**. It indicates tempo by a click or a beep and some models also have a blinking light. Metronomes are available at all music dealers and are a *must* for serious musicians! There are a wide variety from which to choose, including mechanical (which are wound up) and electronic. Models with the blinking or flashing light are definitely helpful for drummers because of the sound factor. Those with an earphone may also be desirable.

For most exercises in this book, there will be a metronome marking. It consists of a note equaling a number (for example, ♩ = 96) and appears just above the time signature. Simply set your metronome to the number and turn it on. This will be the tempo (as in the example, a quarter note will equal 96 beats per minute). In most instances, you will be given a range of numbers from which to choose (i.e., 60–72). It is a good idea to try a slower tempo first (the smaller number) and work up slowly to a faster one. *However, don't hesitate to choose a tempo slower than what is marked!*

GET INTO THE GROOVE

♩ = 56–69 (all lines)

In the next example, always play the ride cymbal with your right hand and the drums with your left.

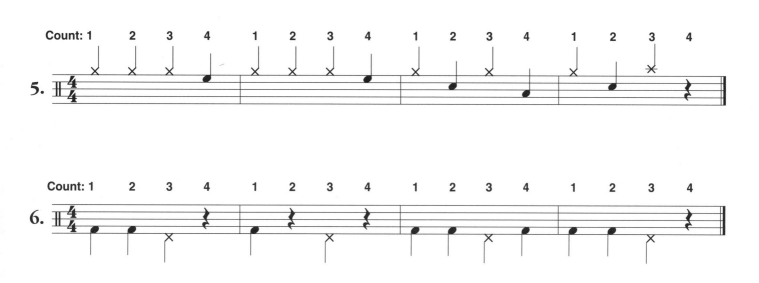

ROCKIN', REELIN', READIN' AND REPEATIN'

The purpose of these next two pages is to gain more skill at reading music—particularly in getting used to where the instruments appear on the staff. (These exercises won't sound much like drum beats.) Don't become frustrated if this takes a little practice. In time, reading music becomes second nature, much like reading the words in this sentence.

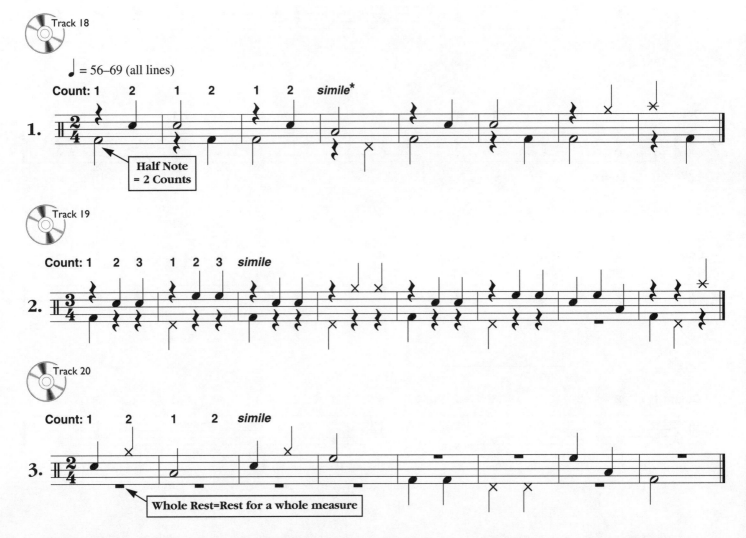

Track 18

♩ = 56–69 (all lines)

Count: 1 2 1 2 1 2 simile*

1.

Half Note = 2 Counts

Track 19

Count: 1 2 3 1 2 3 simile

2.

Track 20

Count: 1 2 1 2 simile

3.

Whole Rest=Rest for a whole measure

*simile—this Italian word indicates to continue in a similar manner. In this book, it is usually applied to counting or sticking (see page 20). Above, you should continue counting as has been established with the pattern.

The dots at the end of the next two lines of music is called a **repeat sign**. When you see this, it signals you to go back to the beginning of the music and repeat it without pause.

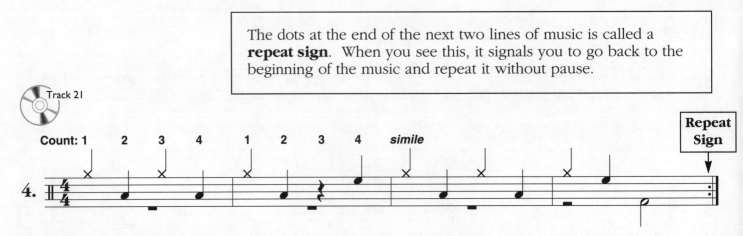

Track 21

Count: 1 2 3 4 1 2 3 4 simile

Repeat Sign

4.

Did you see the repeat sign at the end of line 4 and remember to repeat the music?

MIXIN' IT UP

Here is further reading practice with whole, half and quarter notes and rests. Always count aloud and watch the time signatures. Also, look for lines which have repeat signs at the end!

Whole Note=4 Counts

20

IT TAKES TWO

Whoever said you can't do two things at once? Drummers often play *four* things at one time! Inorder to build to that stage, let's try playing two notes at the same time. Often, the measures in each line are the same with an occasional change. Take it slowly at first and always remember to count as you play. This time the counting is not marked on the page. (If you feel you need it, you can pencil it in above the music. First try counting without marking it, then only mark it where it's needed.) In place of the counting is **sticking**. This indicates which stick to use. An "R" above a note means to play with the right hand; an "L" signifies the left. Try to follow the sticking as you read the music. The stickings marked are only suggestions and are not set in stone.

Prime Time ♩ = 72–84 (all lines)

Cool Waltz

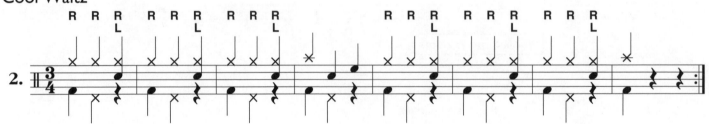

Hail to the Chief (March)

Slavic Backbeat

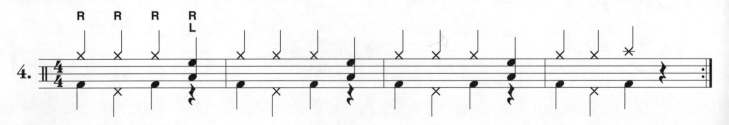

STICK TO IT!

These easy patterns should be fun. As always, counting helps you correctly place the notes and keep a steady tempo.

Swing It!

Double Dip

This next example may require extra effort. After completing the first line, continue without pause to the next line, then the same at the end of the second line (as if the three lines were one long line of music). In music, the single bar at the end of a line indicates to go on to the next line.

Rock Solid

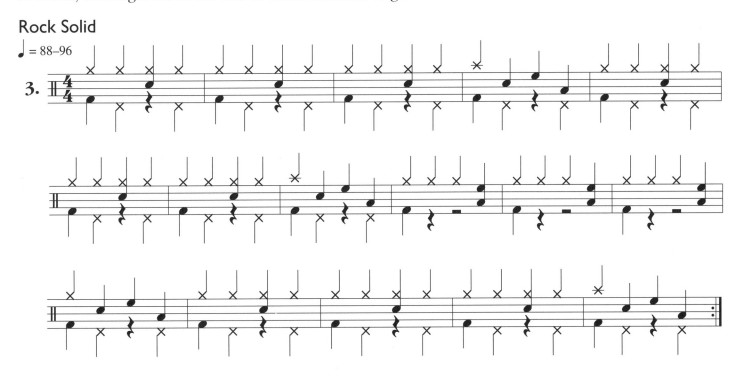

Chops Builder To practice facility in moving about your set, as well as in developing coordination, play the following exercise. Start slowly and very gradually pick up speed. As soon as you feel the least bit of tension in any muscles, begin to gradually slow down. Repeat this four times. The trick is to stay relaxed while keeping the notes evenly spaced!

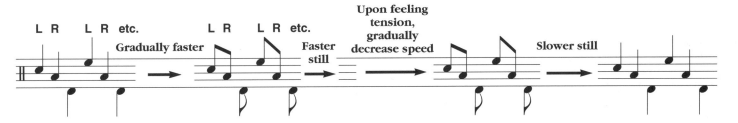

CRAZY EIGHTHS

Up until now, you've been counting on the beat ("one . . . two . . . three . . . " and so forth).
Here, you'll learn to count between the quarter-note beats.

Eighth notes can have a "flag" or can be beamed together in a
series. It is the use of flags or beaming that distinguish the
eighth note from a quarter note.

Flags   **Beams**

A measure of eighth notes in 4/4 time appears like this:

Count them as indicated above ("+" is
spoken as "and"). Now set your
metronome to the tempo indicated. Count
again aloud as your metronome clicks. You must fit the "ands" evenly between the beats,
making it sound smooth.

Try the following line on your set. Count aloud as you play, alternating hands (right, left, right, etc).
The bass drum keeps the beat, like a metronome would.

Notice that in the last bar, there is no need to count "and" after beats three and four. (But you should
still leave the correct spacing between those last two beats as if you were counting "and.")

An eighth rest looks like this: ♪

Try counting, then playing, the following lines which combines eighth notes and rests. The rhythms can
be tricky, so count carefully.

MORE EIGHTHS

This page will give you more experience playing eighth notes while becoming accustomed to "moving around the set." This will assist you in learning to play fills a bit later. The feet play the same pattern in each measure, so you can concentrate on the eighth notes in the hands. Use your metronome. Since stickings are not marked, find stickings that seem naturally comfortable. If you wish, you can jot in the stickings you like for reference when you practice.

Track 26 **Play-Along Instructions**

Track 31 This last line uses only hands. The right hand stays with the ride cymbal, while the left plays the drums.

Did you remember to repeat as marked?

24

LOOK MA, NO HANDS!

Here are some exercises to help develop technique for your feet. You may wish to review page 13, which discusses the various techniques for the bass drum and hi-hat.

Use only the toe technique on hi-hat for this line.

KEEPING TIME

Many of the exercises from here on will consist of the repetition of a measure. The repetition of a stylistic pattern (while not necessarily an *exact* repetition) is known as playing **time**. Some drummers, such as the late big-band drummer Mel Lewis and rocker Charlie Watts (The Rolling Stones), have been known for their ability to "keep great time," rather than using flashy technique. What this really means is that they keep a steady beat and everything they play fits together and sounds appropriate within the context of the music. *Keeping great time is something every drummer should strive for!*

In the exercises below, concentrate by *listening* to your playing. These exercises are kept somewhat simple to enable you to do this.

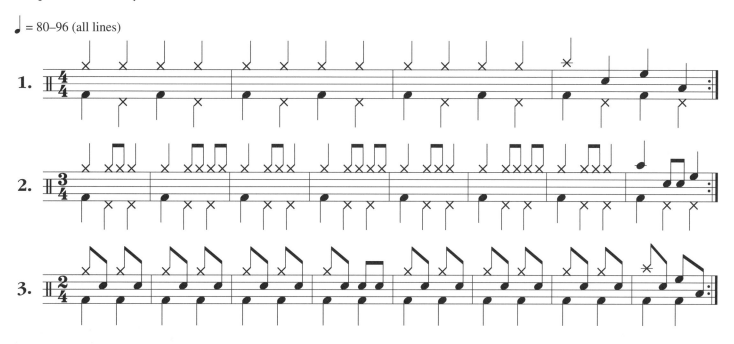

The next exercise is 16 measures. Music often consists of 4-, 8-, 12- and 16-bar **phrases** (small sections of music). This piece actually consists of four groups of four-bar phrases. Line 3 on page 21 is constructed the same way.

 Track 32

Play the ride cymbal pattern on closed hi-hat throughout.

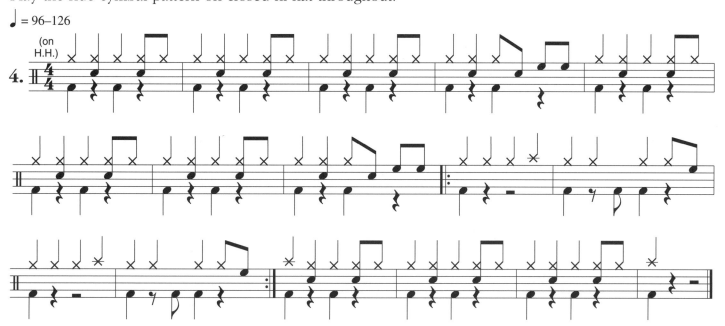

MO', MO', MO'!

You will now learn to play time (patterns) for a few basic styles of music. As you go through this book, you will encounter more patterns for the various styles . . . and they will become more interesting and exciting as your skills develop.

The counting is not marked, but you should still count whenever you have trouble with a measure. The stickings are not marked either, so you may want to pencil in stickings. (The right hand always plays the ride cymbal.)

When a measure is to be played exactly as the one before it, a sign is used indicating this called a **one-bar repeat sign**:

Play the first measure, then play it again as indicated by the repeat sign.

Chops Builder INTRODUCTION TO THE DOUBLE-STROKE ROLL

The first stroke is executed with the wrist and the second is a bounce controlled by the fingers. The goal is to make both strokes equal in volume. Start slowly, then gradually get faster (always keeping the notes even), then start slowing down when you've reached top speed without your muscles tensing up.

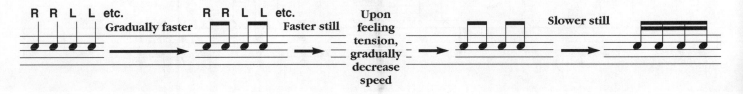

THREE'S COMPANY

You should be ready to progress to playing three notes at one time. This really opens up the possibilities. Again, it is wise to first practice the feet separately, then the hands, combining them afterwards. These exercises are similar to the previous page to help make it easy for you.

Easy Rock

Hard Rock

Two-Step Strut

Ballad

Like the repeat sign, there is a sign to indicate a **two-bar repeat**.

Play the first two bars, then at the two-bar repeat, play the two bars again without pause.

Waltzin' with Wendy

FILL IN THE BLANKS

You may recall from page 25 that music is often composed of phrases (small 4-, 8- or 16-bar sections). Additionally, you might have noticed that many of the lines you've practiced on the last few pages consist of a pattern and, at the end of the line, there is a distinct change from that pattern. This change of pattern is a **fill**. It is a drummer *filling* in a sort of "hole" in the music. Ordinarily this hole occurs at the end of a musical phrase (and other instruments may be filling it up in addition to or instead of the drummer).

The following lines have fills written at the end of the four-bar phrases. Feel free to create your own fills and write them in the blank measure. Your fill may replace the one that is written.

This last exercise utilizes a special technique with the snare drum. The stick is flipped over with the tip or bead keeping contact with the drumhead. The butt end of the stick is raised and brought down to strike the rim.

This technique is sometimes known as a **cross-stick rim shot**. This technique is often used in country, Latin and jazz music, although it can also be heard in rock ballads.

Spanish Groove

✗ =cross-stick rim shot.

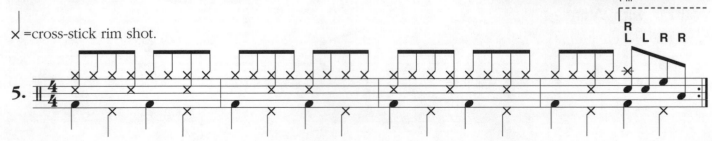

More Basix™

This section continues with the fundamentals of music, drumming technique and various exercises. However, this section moves quickly, so it may take more time to progress through the pages. The key is to *practice carefully*.

Study each page, avoiding the temptation to rush through them. These concepts will require extra effort, so be patient. Above all, do not move ahead to this section unless you feel you've mastered previous pages. Now is a good time to pick out those pages which gave you a bit of trouble and review them for a while. Believe me, it will pay off in the long-run.

NOTE & REST REVIEW

To better understand music notation and the length or duration of notes and rests, the relationship between them should be clear. (You may first wish to review page 10 and the names of the rests and notes.) Remember that for every type of note, there exists a rest of equal length.

	Notes	Rests
One whole note or rest equals two halves:	𝅝 = 𝅗𝅥 𝅗𝅥	▬ = ▬ ▬
One half note or rest equals two quarters:	𝅗𝅥 = ♩ ♩	▬ = 𝄼 𝄼
One quarter note or rest equals two eighths:	♩ = ♫	𝄼 = 𝄾 𝄾
One eighth note or rest equals two sixteenths (discussed on the following page):	♪ = ♬	𝄾 = 𝄿 𝄿

Here's another way to look at the relationship of notes:

SWEET SIXTEENTHS

In order to learn more advanced patterns and fills, it will be necessary to add sixteenth notes and rests to your vocabulary.

Like eighth notes, sixteenths have flags or beams. Rather than one flag or beam, however, sixteenths have two:

Flags   **Beams**

or

A measure of sixteenth notes in various meters follows:

Set your metronome to the tempo indicated, then count as indicated above. Count again aloud as your metronome clicks. You must fit the "e" and "ah" evenly between the eighth beats, making it sound smooth.

Try the following line on your set. Count aloud as you play, alternating hands. The bass drum keeps the beat, like a metronome would.

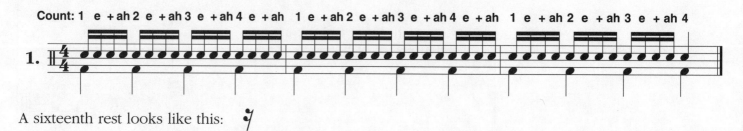

A sixteenth rest looks like this:

Try counting, then playing the following line which combines sixteenth notes and rests:

MORE SIXTEENTHS

Here are more exercises to practice reading sixteenth notes and rests. Be sure to count to become accustomed to these. This is going to take extra time. Note how eighth notes are often beamed to sixteenths. Beams tie together notes within a beat so each beat is visually distinct.

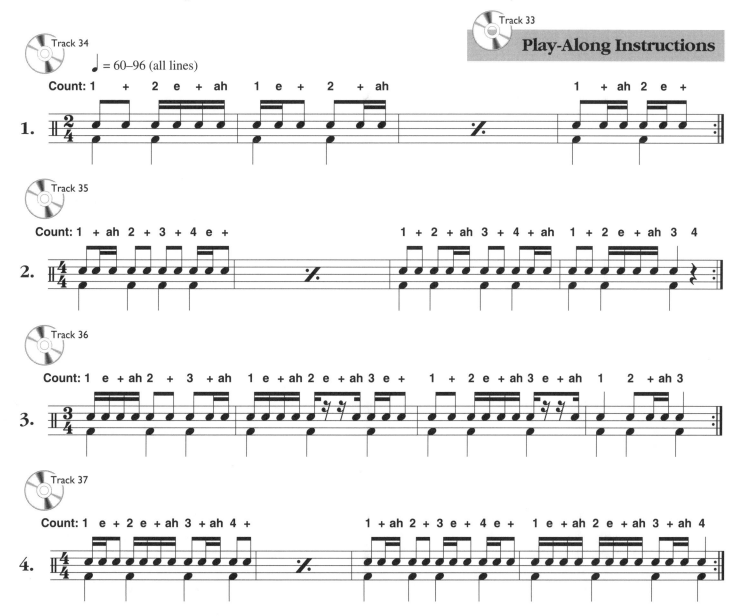

Though counting is not marked, you should be able to count the next lines.

DOTTED RHYTHMS

When a note or rest is followed by a dot, it increases its value by one half. Here are the most frequent dotted-note values you'll come across:

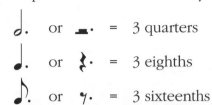

- ♩. or ▬. = 3 quarters
- ♪. or 𝄾. = 3 eighths
- ♬. or 𝄿. = 3 sixteenths

A dot may be applied to *any* note or rest (in addition to those shown above).

Try reading, then practicing, the following lines:

DYNAMICS—WAKING UP THE MUSIC

An element of all music that creates interest is contrast—variations in the music, sometimes subtle, by way of volume, types of sounds (playing on different cymbals and drums), tempo, etc.

Let's examine volume. Pick one of your favorite exercises on the previous page. Try playing it as softly as possible the first time, then play loudly when you repeat it. Here are symbols used in music to indicate the amount of volume to be used. These indications (derived from the Italian language) are known as **dynamics**.

Symbol	Italian	English
pp	*pianissimo*	very soft
p	*piano*	soft
mp	*mezzo piano*	medium soft
mf	*mezzo forte*	medium loud
f	*forte*	loud
ff	*fortissimo*	very loud
◁	*crescendo*	gradually louder
▷	*diminuendo*	gradually softer

There is an additional type of dynamic called an **accent**. This symbol, which resembles a "greater than" sign in math, appears above or below a note.

Notes with accents are played a bit louder than others, usually by one or two dynamic levels. Try this easy exercise.

Accents—play marked notes *f* (loud), one dynamic louder than *mf*.

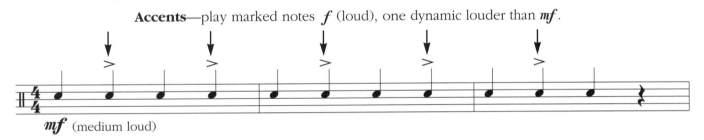

mf (medium loud)

Remember, *an accent ONLY affects the note that is marked.*

An accent may not always mean "loud." Play this exercise.

pp (very soft)

Since this exercise is marked *pp* (very soft), the accented notes are played louder, but should only be *p* (soft) or, at the loudest, *mp* (medium soft).

Accents are used on the next page and throughout the rest of the book. Keep an eye out for them. Like other dynamics, they help bring life to music.

DIGGING IN!

Here are some basic rock-oriented patterns using sixteenths and dotted rhythms. Fills are played in the fourth bar. *The right hand plays on a closed hi-hat, read from the ride-cymbal line.* (Because of this, the hi-hat has been omitted here.) These are tricky, so it may take extra effort until you feel comfortable with them. Also, watch for dynamic markings (see the previous page).

◀ *Keith Moon* (The Who)
Photo: Courtesy of M.C.A.

Keith Moon of The Who was one of the m
influential rock drummers of all time; his
wild, expressive style reflected the general
attitude of freedom and intensity that
characterized the best classic rock of the 19
and 1970s.

HI-HAT TECHNIQUE

Up to this point, all playing on the hi-hat has been with it closed or partially open. It is common to play rhythms on the hi-hat while intermittently opening and closing it. The standard symbol for indicating open hi-hat is **o** and closed is **+**.

Try playing these lines. (The hi-hat is written where the ride cymbal is usually indicated.) The hi-hat need not be opened fully. In fact, this is rarely done. The cymbals only need to be slightly separated in order to create the desired "sizzle" sound.

The degree to which you open the hi-hat depends on the sound you're looking for. Like other aspects of drumming, don't resist experimentation!

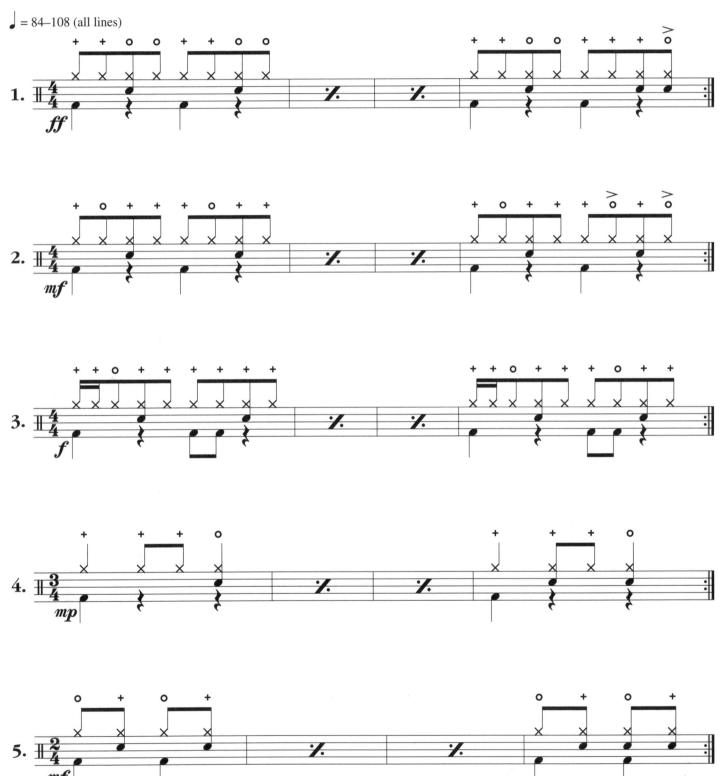

ROLLS

A guitar, trumpet or other instrument can sustain or hold a note. But how does a drummer sustain a sound on a drum? The answer is by playing a **roll.** There are several types of rolls:

Single Stroke
This roll sounds less like a constant, sustained sound and more like fast individual notes. It is often used on low toms and cymbals to sustain sound. On page 9 you saw how this is executed. The roll may be implemented in fills and solos.

Double Stroke
This roll can produce a good sustained sound when played "closed" (fast), but also can resemble the single stroke when played "open" (slow). It is mostly used on the snare and also, to a lesser extent, on the toms, closed hi-hat and cymbals. On page 26 this roll was introduced. The ability to play this roll is especially useful in jazz drumming, but is applicable in rock, too.

Multiple Bounce (sometimes referred to as "buzz," crushed, unmeasured or orchestral roll)

The concept behind this roll is to get many bounces per stick stroke. The bounces are not controlled the way they are with the double-stroke roll. On the drumset, its use is a bit limited. On the next page you will be instructed how to play this roll.

NOTATION

A roll is designated in music by one of two ways:

1) Three diagonal slashes above the note or a combination of slashes and flags equalling three in number (cutting across the stem when there is one).

2) Multiple bounce only—a "z" above the note, cutting across the stem. This notation is rare.

As you can see, the roll is often tied to a note (with a curved line) to indicate on which beat the roll should end.

ROLLIN' OVER

Here are some exercises for the snare drum. Try either the double-stroke or multiple-bounce roll after you've become familiar with it (see bottom of this page).

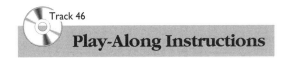

Track 46

Play-Along Instructions

Chops Builder

INTRODUCTION TO THE MULTIPLE-BOUNCE ROLL

To learn this roll, first press the stick into the head loosely enough so there are many rapid bounces. There should be almost no space between each bounce, and it should resemble a "buzz" sound. Do this with each hand.

After practicing this fundamental technique for a few minutes, try the exercise. You should play the "buzz" stroke, alternating hands, attempting to make smooth connections between each stroke.

This is how the roll is played. Continue practicing this, striving to achieve a constant, "seamless" sound.

TRIPLETS

In the context of one beat, you've played two notes (eighths), and four notes (sixteenths), evenly.

Eighths
Two notes per beat (eighth notes):

Sixteenths
Four notes per beat (sixteenth notes):

Now, we will learn three notes per beat—**triplets**. A triplet is a group of three notes played in place of two notes of the same value. Play the following exercise, using the bass drum to keep the beat. Keep the space between the notes even as with eighths and sixteenths.

Eighth-note Triplets
Three notes per beat

Triplets are indicated by a *"3"* above or below the note grouping. The above example utilized eighth-note triplets, but they may exist as quarter-note and sixteenth-notes and other groupings.

To play quarter-note triplets, first think of eighth-note triplets, but play every other one. The following exercise, in which every other note is accented in the first bar, will help you get the feel for the quarter-note triplets in the second bar:

> Brackets are used to indicate groupings where notes are not beamed.

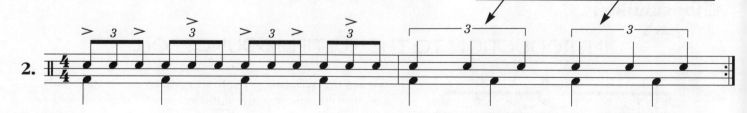

MORE TRIPLETS

These exercises should help you become more familiar with triplets. You may play the bass-drum part on the hi-hat for variety. Be patient and listen to the recording—this page is not easy. Don't overlook dynamics!

Track 52 — **Play-Along Instructions**

PICK-UPS

In all the music you've played in this book, you've begun on beat 1 (or "on the downbeat," as they say). But music doesn't always start on the downbeat. When this occurs, the music is described as having "pick-ups."

When repeating these lines, include the pick-up.

Whatever is missing from the pick-up measure is sometimes found in the last measure. In other words, the first and last "incomplete" measures in a piece together make a complete one. This way of writing music is an old practice that is sometimes still observed. (Don't let it confuse you!)

In the next line, there is a double bar. Do not play the pick-up when you repeat the line. Go to the double bar, which has a repeat sign to indicate where the repeat begins.

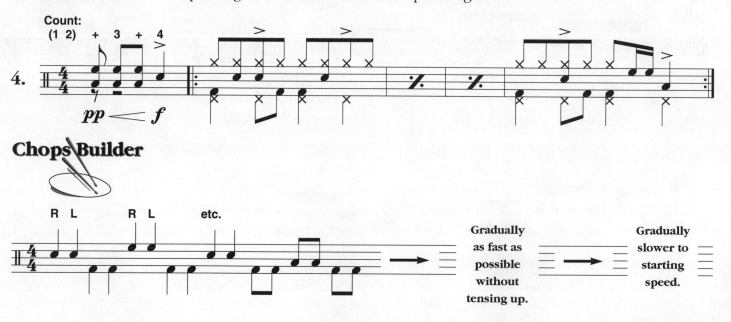

FIRST AND SECOND ENDINGS

Look at line 1. Notice the indications at the end of the line. These are referred to as **first** and **second endings**. Play the line all the way to the repeat sign (at the first ending), repeat as you normally would, but when you reach . . .

The First Ending `1.` ⌐⎯⎯⎯⎯⎯⎯⎯⎯⎯⎯⎯⎯

. . . the second time, do *not* play the music under it. Skip it and play the music under:

The Second Ending `2.` ⌐⎯⎯⎯⎯⎯⎯⎯⎯⎯⎯⎯⎯

To help focus on understanding first and second endings, the following lines are similar to the beats played on the previous page.

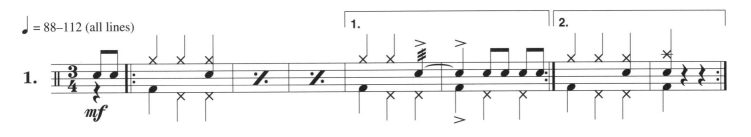

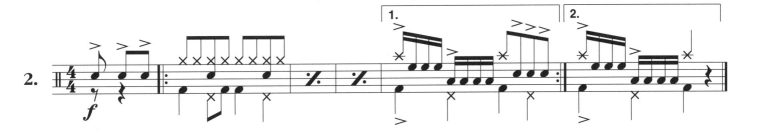

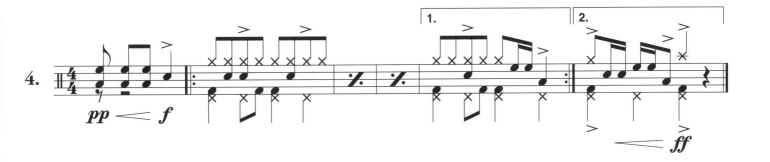

SPECIAL TECHNIQUES

The following techniques are part of a large body of "effects" and patterns known as **rudiments**. These include assorted rolls and certain sticking patterns. It is recommended you purchase *International Drum Rudiments* for further study.

RIM SHOTS

This is *the* loudest effect on drums (with the possible exception of a double rim shot, which is explained below). Simply strike the drum head as you normally would, but angle the stick lower so it strikes the rim simutaneously. Believe me, you'll hear it when you achieve the right sound. In music, a rim shot is often notated with an "x" (like cymbal notes) and "R.S."

A double rim shot is achieved by simultaneous rim shots with both hands and is notated with two "x" noteheads.

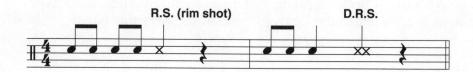

FLAM

This is a rather subtle effect. A "principal" note is played with one hand, but a softer, "grace" note is played a fraction of a second before with the other hand.

It thickens the texture and serves as emphasis to notes—like an accent, but without the added volume.

DRAG

The drag is similar to the flam except there are two softer grace notes played before the principal note:

All of the above effects are more likely to be heard in fills and solo work, though they can be used in other instances. Care should be taken in employing these techniques—if overused, they can become ineffective and bog down the music.

FILLS USING SPECIAL TECHNIQUES

These fills will help you get the feel of how the rim shot, flam and drag may be used. It may take extra effort to master these fills. **These measures are *not*** **designed to be played one after another** as in reading a line of music. Play three measures of a basic beat you've learned in the corresponding time signature, then play the written fill in bar four. For the two-bar fills, play two bars of the basic beat, then the fill. Choose a relaxed tempo at first—one that feels comfortable. The stickings are only suggestions, and you should try your own variations. (Where sticking is not marked, try alternating hands first.)

One-Bar Fills

Two-Bar Fills

SWINGING

Sometimes certain music has a "swing" feel that often employs triplet rhythms. However, the music is generally not written with triplets. As a result, the written music will often include an indication that eighth-note rhythms (or dotted eighths followed by a sixteenth) are to be played as triplets:

As a result, this written rhythm:

or this written rhythm:

is played like:

Look for the indication to "swing" the rhythms in exercises.

PLAYING "SWING" RHYTHMS ON CYMBALS

The "swing" rhythm, which is often played on the ride cymbal or hi-hat, may be executed as shown in the diagram.

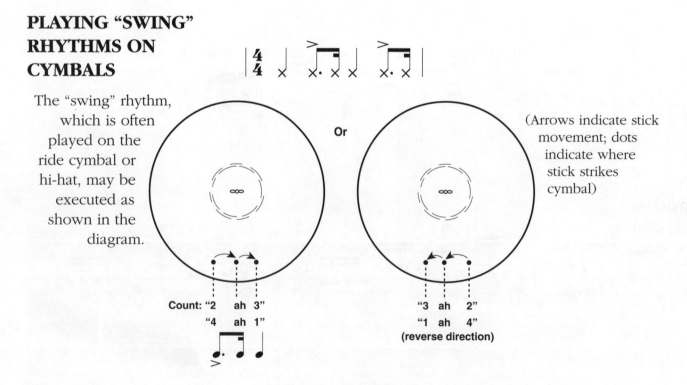

(Arrows indicate stick movement; dots indicate where stick strikes cymbal)

Because of the strong accent on beats 2 and 4 with this jazz-oriented swing pattern, it may feel natural to let the stick bounce to the left or right after playing on beats 2 and 4. This movement is very slight, but helps create a relaxed feel.

Playing Beats & Fills

PART IV

PRACTICING THIS SECTION

The measures in each line on these pages are not meant to be read in succession (with the exception of the SITTING IN pages). They are to be practiced repeating any "pattern" measure three times, followed by a "fill" bar. You can mix the pattern bars with any of the "fill" bars. Where there are two-bar fills, the pattern bar should be played only twice before playing the fill. The idea is to always create four-bar phrases. You can often combine two one-bar fills to create a two-bar fill.

Again, use the methods of practice that have helped you in the past: 1) count rhythms carefully; 2) try combining two or three parts before playing an entire pattern; 3) "hear" the pattern in your head; 4) always stay relaxed. If you take a little extra time to follow these suggestions, it will pay off.

For each style, there are a few familiar songs listed to help you understand how that style sounds rhythmically. You may even want to try playing along to the original recordings of those songs—the performer is listed, rather than songwriter—which are readily available. (The album is not listed because the songs often exist on more than one album.)

For kits larger than four pieces: feel free to experiment using different toms when playing fills. The rhythms can be played on assorted drums and the written fills are only a sample of the style.

SITTING IN and VARIATION Sections
There are play-along pages which coordinate with the recordings, called **"SITTING IN."**

These pages put some of the assorted beats and fills into practice. You may listen to the full recording with the drums, then turn off the right channel and "sit in" as the drummer.

The **"VARIATION"** section at the bottom of some pages will give you more suggestions and ideas to further enhance your playing.

▲ *Ringo Starr* Photo:© T. Eagan

Ringo Starr was an underrated drummer; because he was a member of The Beatles, it is sometimes overlooked that he was also somewhat of a pioneer, being one of the first effective players of the contemporary straight-ahead rock beat.

Early Rock   as in *Johnnie B. Goode* (Chuck Berry) and *Proud Mary* (Creedence Clearwater Revival)

♩ = 100–160

Patterns (One-bar)

(Two-bar)

Fills (One-bar)

(Two-bar)

VARIATIONS

A   Try rim shots on the snare for an extra "kick."

B   Play the hi-hat on all four beats or play the ride cymbal part on closed hi-hat.

C   Instead of constant eighth notes on the ride cymbal, ocasionally mix in quarter notes.

Hard Rock/Metal

as in *Purple Haze* (Jimi Hendrix) and *Welcome to the Jungle* (Guns N' Roses)

VARIATION

Experiment playing with the hi-hat on beats 2 and 4, then on all 4 beats.

Disco/Dance

as in *Thriller* (Michael Jackson) and *Stayin' Alive* (Bee Gees)

The pattern for disco or dance music primarily revolves around the following hi-hat rhythm, which emphasizes the "and" of each beat:

Patterns

A basic beat is created by adding snare and bass as follows:

These next patterns incorporate sixteenths on the hi-hat. First practice snare and hi-hat before adding bass drum.

Patterns 8–10 have the right hand playing only on the "and" of each beat.

Fills

VARIATIONS

A   Play patterns 1–4 without hitting the hi-hat on the beat (only on the off beat.)

B   Practice patterns 8–11 with the hi-hat opening on the offbeat and closing on the beat as in patterns 1–4.

C   Patterns 8–11 may be played with the ride-cymbal part on the bell of the cymbal or closed hi-hat. (for hi-hat, open and closed as in B.)

Reggae (Ska)

as in *Red, Red Wine* (UB40) and recordings of Third World, Peter Tosh, and Bob Marley and the Wailers.

There is always an accent on beats two and four with the bass drum and snare, though it is not marked. As with disco/dance music, the ride cymbal part is played on the hi-hat, which is opened only when indicated.

♩ = 52–76

Patterns

Fills

VARIATIONS

A Use cross-stick rim shot on the snare drum for the patterns, which is very characteristic of this musical style—see page 28.

B Try using some of the disco/dance beats, placing the bass drum on beats 2 and 4 rather than what's written.

C Swing the rhythms a bit (♫ = ♩♪)—see page 44.

Funk   as in *Play That Funky Music* (Average White Band) and *Brick House* (The Commodores)

Of all rock styles, this is the most complex, so you'll need to take extra time with this page. The hi-hat should be used instead of the ride cymbal on patterns 1–3.

Patterns ♩ = 88–112

Fills

....

VARIATIONS

A   Patterns 4–9 may have the ride cymbal part played on hi-hat.

B   Try playing steady eighths, rather than quarters, on hi-hat (with foot).

Rock Shuffle

as in *Doctor My Eyes* (Jackson Browne) and *Just a Gigolo* (David Lee Roth)

Patterns

Fills

SITTING IN

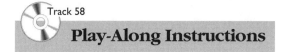

Play-Along Instructions

EARLY ROCK ('60s) *use any patterns and fills from page 46*

You'll note on the recording that the drummer plays quarter notes on partially open hi-hat until measure 25, then the ride cymbal is played near the bell with a mixture of quarter and eighth notes. There is no count off for "Jess's Night Out" since the guitar sets the tempo, and notice there are pick-ups at the beginning .

When there are **multiple bars of consecutive rests**, there is a type of shorthand to indicate this (rather than having several measures of whole rests). For example, eight bars of rests are indicated as:

8

The number above this extended rest indication tells you how many measures to rest. You'll see this at the beginning of "Jess's Night Out."

Jess's Night Out

P. Wilson

At the end of "Jess's Night Out," is a ***fermata*** (pause sign); another music term derived from the Italian language. This indicates to hold a note for an unspecified length beyond the note's value. An accepted rule of thumb is to hold the note at least 1-1/2 times its value. The fermata is encountered most often at the end of music, but also may occur at the end of a music section.

SITTING IN

 Track 60

METAL *use patterns 1, 2 & 6-9 and fills 3 & 5 from page 47*

On the recording, the drummer uses a very active sixteenth-note pattern on the bass drum, which follows the bass guitar line. It is very effective, but any of the more basic patterns mentioned above will work. As "Shattered Iron" is driven by a sixteenth-note feel, sixteenth-note fills are desirable. Notice the frequent downbeat cymbal crashes on the recording, typical of this drumming style.

The term **ad lib.** (from the Latin *ad libitum*) simply means in modern usage to be creative. When written in music, it often indicates to elaborate on a given pattern, playing what seems to fit within the context of the music. You'll see this at the end of "Shattered Iron," letting the drummer know to create a solo.

Shattered Iron

P. Wilson

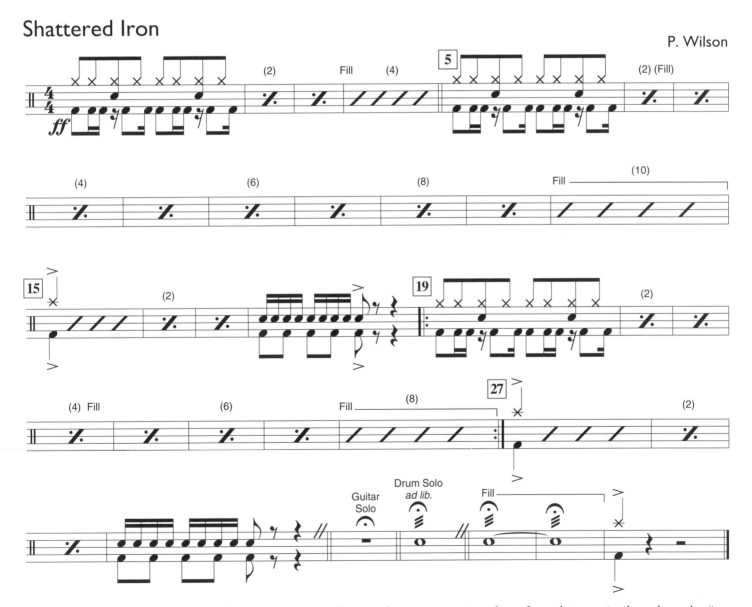

Note the slashes at the end of measures 30 and 32. These are curiously referred to as "railroad tracks." They indicate to halt the tempo, making a break or cut off before going ahead.

SITTING IN

Track 61

REGGAE *use any patterns and fills from page 49; be sure to "swing" the rhythms (see page 44).*

On the recording, the drummer adds cowbell (mounted on the bass drum) on the repeat as interplay with the hi-hat rhythm, then uses the bell of the cymbal and, finally, returns to hi-hat. Throughout the tune, there are lively punctuations within the pattern to add rhythmic interest. **Note**: the count off on the recording equals *eighths*, not quarter notes ("1 - 2 - 3 - 4" = "1 + 2 +").

Better Way, Brighter Day

P. Wilson

◀ **Stewart Copeland**
Photo: Lissa Wales

As drummer of the late 1970s and 1980s supergroup The Police, the brilliant Stewart Copeland introduced reggae rhythms to a generation of punk and new wave rock fans.

Track 62

FUNK *use any patterns and fills from page 50*

Basically, "Reflex" is a tune without a melodic line. The drummer uses a mixture of syncopated rhythms on the recording revolving around a sixteenth-note pattern.

Reflex

P. Wilson

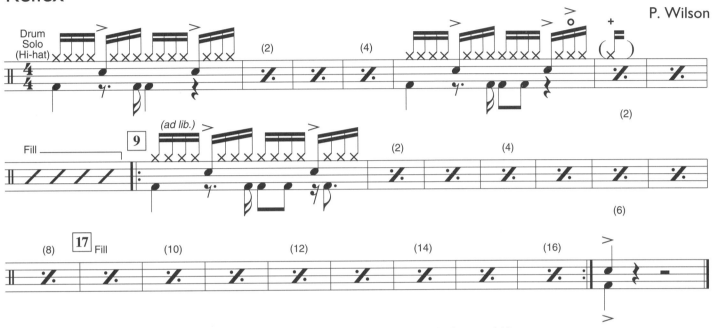

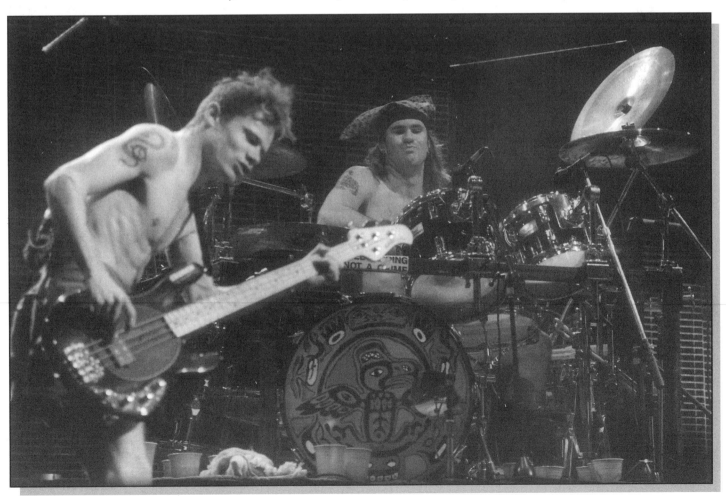

▼ **Chad Smith** (Red Hot Chili Peppers)
Photo: Lissa Wales

The Red Hot Chili Peppers are perhaps best known for their powerful-but-precise grooves, for which Chad Smith's explosive drumming serves as a foundation.

PART V Odds & Ends

WHAT TO PLAY (SELECTING YOUR INSTRUMENTS)

ACOUSTIC DRUMS

A drumset consists of four elements: drums, cymbals, hardware (stands, mounting devices and pedals) and a stool or "throne." For your first set, you will need at least the following:

Drums

Snare—a relatively small drum, characterized by snares (almost always wire) stretched across the bottom head. A lever on the side of the drum releases or engages the snares. (Releasing them creates, in effect, a somewhat high-pitched tom.)

Tom-tom (or "tom")—a mid-sized drum, pitched somewhere between the snare and bass. It is highly preferable, though not essential, to have at least two toms: one mounted on the bass drum and the other, larger one a "floor tom," which usually has self-contained hardware. (Another practical arrangement for positioning tom-toms includes racks.)

Bass—the largest drum, which sits on the floor and is played with a pedal.

Cymbals

Ride—a large, relatively thick cymbal (19 to 22 inches in diameter).

Crash—a mid-sized cymbal (16 to 18 inches in diameter) with a quick response and often a rather quick decay when struck hard. If your budget does not allow for this cymbal, you may get by without it, but it will be *sorely* missed and should be added at the first opportunity.

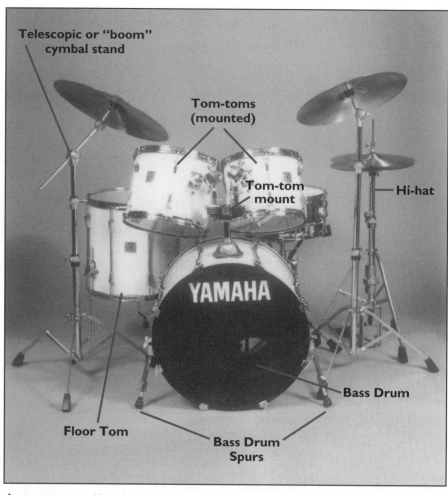

▲ *Acoustic Set (front).*

Hi-Hat—a set of two rather small cymbals (13 to 15 inches in diameter) which can vary in weight/thickness, depending on the desired sound. Sometimes the bottom cymbal is slightly thicker than the top.

Hardware

Snare Stand—obviously, to support the snare drum.

Cymbal Stands—one for the ride, the other for the crash. (On some older sets, hardware for a ride-cymbal stand is attached to the bass drum.) Wing nuts, with felt washers placed above and below the cymbal, keep them from flying off the stand. Small plastic sleeves, which fit around the threads at the top of the stand, keep bare metal from touching bare metal, preventing the cymbal

from cracking (see page 60 on care and maintenance). Telescopic stands, or "boom" stands, are often used for larger, heavier cymbals and allow greater flexibility when positioning them.

Hi-Hat Stand—a particular cymbal stand with a tension spring in its shaft (which is usually adjustable) and a foot pedal to lower the top cymbal onto the bottom one. A "clutch" and felt pads hold the top cymbal on a rod which moves with the pedal; the lower cymbal rests on another felt pad and holder. The stand includes an adjustment on the bottom cymbal holder to offset the angle of the lower cymbal. This prevents the two cymbals from locking together in a vacuum (airlock) when they are brought together with the pedal.

Crash Cymbal

Ride Cymbal

Snare

Hi-Hat angle adjust-ment

Hi-Hat tension adjust-ment

Stool

Hi-Hat Pedal

Bass Drum Beater

Bass Drum Pedal

Bass Drum pedal tension adjustment

▲ *Acoustic Set (back).*

The bottom cymbal is available with drilled holes to alleviate airlock.

Tom-Tom Mount—holds the tom in place and is generally connected to the bass drum shell. In the case of a floor tom, rods or "legs" elevate it off the floor.

Bass Drum Pedal—connects, via a clamp, to the rim of the bass drum.

Bass Drum Spurs—two rods which keep the drum from tilting side to side or creeping forward.

Miscellaneous

Stool or ***Throne***—a small padded seat with height adjustment.

Rug or ***Mat***—necessary for protecting the floor, as well as the

bass drum bottom. It also keeps the bass drum from creeping forward following each impact of the pedal's beater, so choose something that will not slide on a smooth surface.

Sticks—a possible beginner size is "5A" or "5B," but anything in that range is good. (Note: There is no standard system for classifying assorted stick types.) However, a stick bigger than "2B" is too clumsy. It is wise to resist selecting too small a stick because the muscles in the fingers, hands and wrist will better develop with a little weight. In addition, the slightly heavier stick will bounce higher (beneficial!) and last a little longer. Sticks with plastic nylon tips were created to give a more articulated sound on cymbals,

and they also protect the wood tip. Sticks with or without nylon tips are both fine, but realize that each one creates a different type of sound, particularly on cymbals. When purchasing sticks, check for warped wood by rolling them on a flat surface (which most reputable dealers should allow you to do).

Metronome—see page 16.

Cases (optional)—if you will be moving your drums around to gigs and rehearsals, these will greatly cut down on wear and tear, make storage easier, keep hardware organized and assist with transporting equipment.

Rack Stands (optional)—depending on the amount of additional equipment you have, this hardware can be substituted for several single stands as it is capable of holding several toms and sometimes cymbals too.

Drum Key or ***Lug Wrench*** (a must!)—the purpose of this small tool is to turn the lugs, pulling the drum hoop to tighten the drumhead or loosening it to remove one (see page 61). While it is a bit more expensive, the advantage of a wrench is that it's easier on the hands and easier to use.

Gloves (optional)—some drummers, especially heavy metal players, sport athletic gloves (often the kind weight lifters use to protect their hands and give them a better grip when the hands perspire). Drummers whose hands perspire quite a bit may want to consider trying them out. Realize that gloves can also function as a fashion statement for the player (whether your hands get slippery or not). If you like the idea, use them while you practice in order to get used to playing with them.

ELECTRONIC DRUMS

You will need the equivalent of the basic acoustic drum sounds (see two previous pages), so a set of three or four pads will be necessary in place of the corresponding acoustic drums. Cords are plugged into output jacks on the pads which connect to a "brain." The brain is the synthesizer that creates the various sounds triggered by playing on the pads. The brain connects to an amplifier, which in turn is connected to headphones or speakers in order to hear the sounds. Cymbals will be the same as an acoustic setup (though if you're really into an electronic sound, the cymbals may be pads too). Hardware will differ only where the pads are concerned, but will function similarly. A rug or mat is still recommended, and choice of sticks is the same for both electronic and acoustic drums, although plastic-tipped sticks will have no effect if pads are use for cymbal sounds.

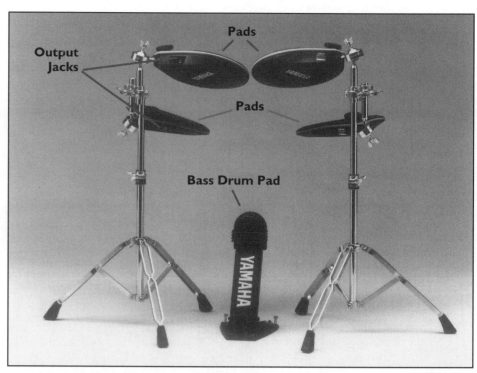

▲ *5-Piece Electronic Drum Set (minus hi-hat).*

BUYING EQUIPMENT (New Versus Used)

There are two rather obvious ways to acquire the instruments: purchasing new equipment from a dealer or buying it used from a dealer or private individual.

In either case, it is always wise to shop around and to avoid "off brands." Buying name brands will help greatly should any hardware need maintenance or replacing.

The advantage in working with a reputable dealer is the service. Such a dealer can assist you with questions you may later have, such as setting up equipment, and can replace faulty merchandise since a warranty is usually provided. If you purchase from a private party, it may be advisable to have setting up and tearing down the set demonstrated, as well as checking the equipment thoroughly. (Imagine the disappointment after handing over the money and driving home to try out your set only to discover you can't put it together!) When shopping used, check to see that all hardware operates and is in good condition (no bent screws, rust, stripped threads, etc.).

▼ *Matt Sorum* (Guns 'n' Roses)
Photo: Courtesy of Yamaha

Drummer Matt Sorum anchors the hard rock group Guns n' Roses with his consistently solid and powerful beats.

KEEPING YOUR EQUIPMENT IN SHAPE

Drum upkeep doesn't require much effort provided your set is in good shape to begin with. First, you should become familiar with the parts of a drum.

Probably the most regular effort will consist of changing the heads when they are worn or broken (see the next page for a guide on changing them). At this time, it is good to check for bent screws, broken snares, warped rims, faulty strainers and cracked shells. The screws should be clean and have a light coat of lubricant (such as a light grade of oil or grease, silicone spray or a dab of Vaseline).

The pedals for the bass drum and hi-hat require occasional lubrication. Once or twice a year for sets played regularly is often sufficient.

It is a good habit to cover your set when it's not in use. (This is assuming you will keep it set up in an area for daily practice and not tear it down, placing it in cases every day!) An old, but clean, sheet will protect it from dust and dirt.

The cymbals need little attention outside of an occasional polish. However, NEVER use an abrasive cleaner. There is cymbal cleaner made for polishing, but it is surprising what a little non-abrasive soap and elbow grease will do. It is important to regularly check the felts and plastic sleeves on the stands to see that they protect the cymbal from contact with the stand. *Not having the sleeves and felts can lead to a crack in your cymbal!*

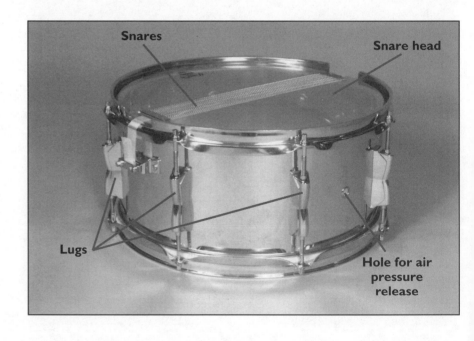

REPLACING A DRUMHEAD

The first time you break a drumhead it may seem catastrophic. You can't do much of anything on your set until the head is replaced. If you are really fearful of doing fix-it type work, one option is taking it to a music repair dealer for replacement.

If you are serious about being a drummer, however, it will be necessary—and really not so hard!—to learn how to replace a drumhead. You will need to measure the head size and specify whether it's a batter head (the side you play upon) or snare head (the *underside* of a snare drum). Heads are available in different weights and thicknesses. You may want to consult your music dealer for suggested replacement, depending on the type of drum and the sort of sound you want. Following these steps will make changing a head relatively painless:

1) With your drum key (or a drum wrench), loosen all the screws, but do not pull the screws out of the hoop.

2) Lift the hoop away from the shell leaving the screws hanging loose in the hoop holes.

3) Remove the bad head from the shell.

4) Check wood-shell rims for any imperfections. Take it to a service professional for correction rather than attempting to sand it (which will ruin the rim).

5) Wipe the shell clean with an *only slightly* damp, clean cloth. Wipe it again with a dry cloth. (It may be a good idea to turn the drum upside down and shake it a bit to get rid of any foreign objects or dust inside.)

6) Place the new head on the rim, making sure it fits firmly against the rim.

7) Place the hoop over the head, again making sure it fits snugly over the head.

8) With your fingers, screw the screws into place. (If needed, clean and lubricate the screws with grease or a dab of Vaseline before replacing). The screws should be tightened only with slight finger pressure.

9) Selecting any lug, start tightening the screws making two full turns with the drum key or wrench, working in a pattern across the drum as shown: called cross-tension tuning.

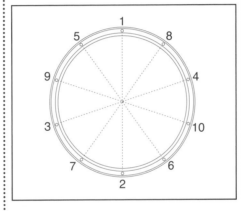

10) Repeat this pattern. If it seems two full turns may be too much, reduce it to one or one-and-a-half turns.

11) Repeat this pattern as much as is necessary to achieve the correct tension, reducing the amount of the turn at each lug with each repetition of the pattern. Between each pattern, apply pressure with your palm in the center of the head in order to let the head "seat" with the edge of the drum. Check the tension by tapping the drumhead.

Fine tuning can be done by tapping at the edge of the drum near each individual lug. Lightly place your finger to eliminate unwanted overtones. Listen to the pitch. If it is higher than the others, loosen the lug slightly, apply pressure to the head momentarily with your palm and tap again. If it is lower in pitch, tighten the lug slightly. Continue tapping and adjusting until the pitch is the same at each lug. When this process is completed, you're ready to get back to playing! (Note: It is normal for the drumhead to stretch a bit over time, so you may want to check your drum and fine tune once a day until the stretching stabilizes over a few days.)

One final note: There is often the fear that when you tighten a head, it's going to pop like a balloon because of crackle sounds. This almost never happens. Heads are tested to withstand an enormous amount of pull. In the rare occurrence that you tighten a head and it breaks, the head may have been defective to begin with. Consider taking it back to the dealer and asking for a replacement.

▲ *Gina Schock* (Go-Go's)
Photo: Courtesy I.R.S.

The Go-Go's were one of the most popular bands of the 1980s, and Gina Schock's rock-steady drumming kept the music fresh and danceable.

TUNING

There are almost as many approaches to tuning drums as there are players. It is a very important consideration since it has much to do with creating "your sound." Because it is a personal preference, no one can tell you how your drums should be tuned. The type of heads you use (discussed next), muffling (see next page), the type of music you play and your own taste will be factors. However, there are some tips that may help you achieve the sound you are looking for. As with other aspects of drumming, much will be accomplished through experimentation.

First, it is desirable to have even tension at each lug. Any turning of a screw should be duplicated with all screws (assuming that there is even tension across the head to begin with). To check this, slightly muffle the drumhead with your finger at the center and tap close to the rim at each point where there is a screw. (The opposite head should be completely muffled and if you're checking the snare, the snares should be off.) If the pitch is the same, there is even tension. At those points where the pitch is lower or higher, tighten or loosen the screw to match pitches. Do this with both heads on each drum.

You will want to consider the relationship of pitches between each drum. Ordinarily, the snare is the highest pitched drum and the bass drum is the lowest. One approach would be to first find the sounds you like with these two drums, then tune the toms between the snare and bass. (If you have a large set with many toms, you may want the smallest tom equal to or even higher than the snare, but this would be a rather exceptional situation.) The toms are tuned highest to lowest with respect to their size.

You may not want to tune both heads on a drum to the same pitch. On the snare drum, it is usually preferable to tune the top batterhead lower than the snarehead. With toms, tuning the top head higher than the bottom will make the pitch bend upward. Tuning the top head lower than the bottom creates more projection of the drum sound. The common approach with the bass drum heads is to tune the head that is played upon higher in pitch than the front head. Again, there are no hard-and-fast rules, so experiment.

DRUMHEADS

Drumheads are available in different weights and styles. As with tuning, the type of music played and sound desired, along with the volume at which the drummer tends to play, will be deciding factors in the choice of heads.

Thin heads have more attack and tone, and project more, than thick heads. Thick heads have less projection, but a dull attack and little ring. (Of course, the amount of ring can be modified with muffling.) A thicker head will endure heavier playing more than thin heads. As you would expect, medium heads characteristically fall in the middle.

Over the years, special heads, such as "hydraulic" (containing fluid to dampen sound), sound dots (a round dampening patch in the center) and pin stripes (which is a sort of two-ply head) have been manufactured. Generally, transparent and smooth-coated white heads are favored by many because of their superior tone. Jazz drummers often use a rough-coated batterhead on the snare for effective use of brushes.

REMOVING BOTTOM HEADS

You've probably seen drummers who play sets with the bottom heads removed on toms as well as the front of bass drums. This creates a sound which is less resonant (generally speaking). It also makes tuning the drums simpler because there is one less head to deal with. If you want less "ringing" to your kit, experiment by removing the bottom head to one of your toms. Once you fiddle with the tuning of one tom with the bottom head removed and decide you like that sound, you may want to take the time to try it with the remaining toms and bass drum.

Bon Jovi set the standard for hard-rock pop music in the 1980s, and the tasteful,
energetic drumming of Tico Torres became one of the group's trademarks.

MUFFLING

Many drums include some device to deaden the ring of a drum. Use of these devices are solely up to you based on the type of sound you prefer. There are a few drummers who also will use tape as a method to dampen sound further. The net effect is an extremely dry sound with almost no ring. One big drawback to this is the sticky residue left on the head should the player change his or her mind.

Almost all drummers will apply some dampening to the bass drum. This may involve pillows inside the drum, removing the front head, using factory-made dampening rings, cloth strips fixed to one or both heads with tape, front drumheads with a hole "built-in," as well as tape. Again, you should experiment to see what fits your sound.

One further note, should you ever want to record in a studio, dampening will be a prime consideration. Every kit requires careful microphone placement, combined with close attention to muffling techniques.

HOW TO DEAL WITH NOISE

The biggest curse of your new-found love is that everyone else seems to hate the noise! You will probably want to maintain a practice schedule during times when it is least offensive to others—or you'll be *told* to do so by newfound enemies!

Here are a few suggestions that may help you from becoming the least popular person in your living space, if not the neighborhood:

—Muffle your drums with cloth and tape or just tape applied to the heads; cymbals can be deadened with duct or masking tape. (Realize, however, that the

glue on the tape may be a bit difficult to clean off later.)

—It is common to remove the front bass drum head and place a pillow inside, either leaving the head off or replacing it.

—Use commercial rubber practice pads to muffle the sound (instead of cloth or tape). These pads can be placed on top of the

drums, and are very easy to throw on or off the drums.

—"Soundproof" your practice area by hanging old carpets, blankets or other acoustic material on the walls.

—Use a commercial practice pad set. The added cost for this set will be offset by less wear on your "real" drumset.

WHERE TO GO FROM HERE

FINDING A TEACHER

If you are hooked on learning to play and are considering taking lessons, here are some things to ask yourself and others when selecting a teacher:

1) Does the teacher have experience in teaching and playing?

2) How many students study with the teacher? Can you speak with any of the students currently studying with the teacher? How do they feel about the instruction they've received?

3) Are there professional musicians or teachers who recommend the teacher?

4) What are the fees for the instruction? Are there any discount "packages" that the teacher offers?

Living in a large city will give you more options in your search. Take your time. If you don't feel comfortable with the teacher after a few lessons, for whatever reason, you may want to try another instructor.

ATTEND CLINICS

In larger cities at music stores and at universities, workshops and clinics may occasionally be held. Big-name artists sometimes appear at these seminars, sharing their valuable knowledge. Check with the music stores and the music department at universities in your area to see if they have plans to hold a drumset clinic.

READ DRUM AND MUSIC MAGAZINES

There are several magazines available, either through subscription or purchase your local music dealer you further you skills Magazines (such as *Modern Drummer*) include interviews with artists, playing tips, new equipment info, question and answer columns, etc. But don't overlook other magazines, w valuable drummers a

JOIN P.A.S.

The Percus internatio committed to the education of percussionists and drummers, from beginner to professional. Membership includes a subscription to *Percussive Notes*

magazine, admittance to the P.A.S.I.C. (the annual international convention that is held in a different major city each year) and more. If you ever have the opportunity to attend the P.A.S.I.C., the exposure to several days of clinics with the world's top drummers and percussionists, unusual concerts and the latest equipment is simply overwhelming. For more information, write to P.A.S., 701 NW Ferris, Lawton, OK, USA 73507.

T OTHER ROOKS

books available to help you continue your studies local music deal in finding